SEASONS OF LIFE

SEASONS OF LIFE

KURT BROADNAX

J MERRILL

J MERRILL

J Merrill Publishing, Inc.
434 Hillpine Drive
Columbus, OH 43207
www.JMerrill.pub

Library of Congress Control Number: 2023920307
ISBN-13: 978-1-961475-06-9 (Paperback)
ISBN-13: 978-1-961475-07-6 (eBook)

Book Title: Seasons of Life
Author: Kurt Broadnax

CONTENTS

INTRODUCTION

The inspiration for this book comes from the Bible: Ecclesiastes, Chapter 3, verses 1–11. Humanity faces seasons of life that are common to mankind. We must learn to adjust, adapt, and manage change, knowing God will help us. Let's make adjustments and keep going.

We mature and develop through the seasons of life. Our outlook and perspective are developed through these same seasons.

> *"But the God of all grace, who hath called us unto his eternal glory by Christ Jesus, after ye have suffered a while, make you perfect, stablish, strengthen, settle you."*

— 1 PETER 5:10

People love certain aspects of the seasons, but those same seasons also have elements that people hate. For example, one may love the rebirth of spring, which turns dormant brown grass into luscious green and causes flowers and trees to bloom. However, the pollen in the air may cause significant health issues and discomfort, inevitably leading to a longing for summer.

One may crave relief from hot summer temperatures with the cooler temperatures of autumn, which reveal many colors as leaves change. Yet the beauty of autumn quickly vanishes into a sea of brown, making us crave the holidays that winter brings as well.

Similarly, our spiritual lives mirror the fluctuations we experience throughout the seasons. One day veers in one direction, and the next follows an entirely different course. We must realize that the seasons of life Solomon portrays are not confined by duration. Time can be measured in seconds, minutes, hours, days, weeks, months, years, etc. Therefore, what we experience can last for a brief period or longer than we expect. The more pressing issue is how we respond to the season of life in which we find ourselves.

The danger we face during seasons of trial is blaming God for our pain and misfortune, whining, and becoming so shortsighted that we miss the big picture of His sovereignty. In these moments, we must remember the promises that Scripture declares:

> *"When thou passest through the waters, I*
>   *will be with thee; and through the*
>   *rivers, they shall not overflow thee:*
>   *when thou walkest through the fire,*
>   *thou shalt not be burned; neither shall*
>   *the flame kindle upon thee. For I am*
>   *the Lord thy God, the Holy One of*
>   *Israel, thy Saviour"*

— ISAIAH 43:2–3

All of this is God's wonderful plan for your life. The problem, of course, is that it's not our plan. If given the chance to plan our lives, we would experience no unpleasantness. However, that would be detrimental. God knows that people who are shielded from everything almost invariably become unbearable: selfish, cruel, shallow, and unprincipled. God sends these challenges so that we might learn. There is a time for everything.

A. In Solomon's effort to understand the "true meaning of life," he observes that good times and bad times come to all, repeating themselves in each successive generation.

  1. This process repeats itself with such certainty that Solomon concludes Ecclesiastes 3:15.
  2. The wise man will understand this and prepare for life's ups and downs.

B. Solomon will remind us in Ecclesiastes 3 that things are beyond our control.

1. For example, no matter how rich and powerful, he cannot prevent sorrow, sickness, and death.
2. Solomon will help us see genuine comfort and happiness come only by trusting God.

C. In our text for study in this lesson (Ecclesiastes 3:1–15), we will see Solomon contemplating the providence of God.

> *To everything there is a season, and a time*
> *to every purpose under the heaven.*

— VERSE 1

CHAPTER ONE

TIMES AND SEASONS APPOINTED BY GOD

THESE WORDS ARE MEANT for every person, place, and circumstance. God has appointed the times and seasons, the events of our lives—the happy and the sad, the easy and the difficult.

This notion can evoke worry; it should instill hope, as we know God is in control. God exalts and humbles the same individual. He raises nations and brings them down. Even the day of our death has been set.

GOD IS IN CONTROL

Man has free will. Man's free will can be destructive if it isn't submitted to the will of God. Man's will alone leads to moral decay. Man's will alone can lead to lust, greed, and all kinds of sin. God's word teaches us the best way to live. God's word will be fulfilled. God's word speaks of future events. God's word speaks of evil being removed forever. God's word speaks of Jesus coming back. God's word speaks of a new heaven and a new earth.

GOD'S PURPOSE

Even if we struggle to understand, God has a purpose in what He does. Romans 8:28 reads, *"And we know that all things work together for good to them that love God, to them who are the called according to his purpose."* No matter what occurs, we can trust in God's timing.

This list comprises opposites: fourteen are positive, and fourteen are negative. The fact that Solomon used such extreme opposites and began his list with birth and death is highly significant. Solomon intended to affirm that all our constructive and destructive activities and all His responses to people, objects, and events occur in His timing.

Positive events parallel negative ones to reflect reality. Life isn't solely about beauty and happiness; there's also pain and loss. Life undoubtedly includes laughter and joy but also has a somber side.

Every individual and every creature that comes into existence also passes away. We step onto the stage of life, are physically present for a time, and then our bodies give way. Similarly, Psalm 90 states, *"The days of our years are threescore years and ten; and if by reason of strength they be fourscore years."*

In this ever-changing world, only God can give meaning to life; He alone is unchanging. He directs the chaotic events that seem to lack rhyme or reason.

Ecclesiastes 3:1–8

1. If we live long enough, we will come to know all the items Solomon has mentioned here.
2. Solomon confirms his assertion in Chapter Two that wealth, wisdom, and success are not in human hands.
3. Note how James puts it in James 4:13–16: *"Go to now, ye that say, Today or tomorrow we will go into such a city, and continue there a year, and buy and sell, and get gain: Whereas ye know not what shall be on the morrow. For what is your life? It is even a vapor, that appeareth for a little time, and then vanisheth away. For that ye ought to say, If the Lord will, we shall live, and do this, or that. But now ye rejoice in your boastings: all such rejoicing is evil."*
4. There is a time.

CHAPTER TWO

TO BE BORN AND DIE

OUR BIRTH AND INEVITABLE DEATH

OUR BIRTH IS outside our control, and concerning death, we cannot prevent it. Hebrews 9:27 states, *"And as it is appointed unto men once to die, but after this, the judgment."*

There is a time to be born, usually expected and experienced, with a sense of hope and joy.

CONTRAST OF BIRTH AND DEATH

In contrast, birth and death each have appointed seasons, which come to pass without human interference.

There is also a time to die. Today, we recognize that a beloved friend or family member has passed.

ACKNOWLEDGMENT AND CELEBRATION

It's crucial to recognize, acknowledge, and celebrate a birth. Equally, it's important to celebrate the life of the person who has passed.

ACCEPTANCE AS A JOURNEY

Life itself is a journey; likewise, accepting the reality of death is also a journey, experienced incrementally and often painfully but undoubtedly necessary.

LAST WORDS OF JESUS

Some of Jesus' last words to those He loved deeply were about death. Knowing His death was imminent, He sought to comfort His loved ones. John 14:1–3, 6 reads: *"Let not your heart be troubled: ye believe in God, believe also in me. In my Father's house are many mansions: if it were not so, I would have told you. I go to prepare a place for you. And if I go and prepare a place for you, I will come again, and receive you unto myself; that where I am, there ye may be also. I am the way, the truth, and the life: no man cometh unto the Father, but by me."*

THE GREAT QUESTION

One of the critical questions about death is, "What happens afterward?" The Apostle Paul wrote that to be absent from the body is to be present with the Lord. How will we meet Him?

> *Blessed be the God and Father of our Lord Jesus Christ, which according to his abundant mercy hath begotten us again unto a lively hope by the resurrection of Jesus Christ from the dead, To an inheritance incorruptible, and undefiled, and that fadeth not away, reserved in heaven for you, Who are kept by the power of God through faith unto salvation ready to be revealed in the last time. Wherein ye greatly rejoice, though now for a season, if need be, ye are in heaviness through manifold temptations: That the trial of your faith, being much more precious than of gold that perisheth, though it be tried with fire, might be found unto praise and honour and glory at the appearing of Jesus Christ.*

> — 1 PETER 1:3–7

CHAPTER THREE

TO PLANT AND PLUCK UP THAT WHICH IS PLANTED

THE FARMER'S WISDOM

ANY FARMER CAN ATTEST to the truth of this statement.

SURVIVAL THROUGH AGRICULTURE

Survival depends on knowing when to plant or pluck.

SPIRITUAL IMPLICATIONS

Scriptures for reference:

- *Luke 8:11–15*
- *Matthew 15:13*

What sacrifice are you willing to make for your harvest? If we do nothing, we gain nothing. Where there is no investment, there is no return. Every venture has a starting point and must be developed through a defined process. Without a plan, purpose, and process, we cannot enjoy the fruits of our labor. Our dreams must be transformed into reality.

To make a dream a reality often requires partners who can aid in creativity, development, and production. God provides us with ideas, but we need like-minded individuals to help us realize them. We can't reap what we haven't sown; without application, there will be no results.

God established the principle of sowing and reaping, which can work to our advantage when appropriately understood.

One needs motivation, patience, perseverance, determination, focus, and hard work for success. In due time, we will reap our rewards. Consider the following scriptures for further insight:

> *Even so faith, if it hath not works, is dead,*
> *being alone.*

> — JAMES 2:17

While the earth remaineth, seedtime and harvest, and cold and heat, and summer and winter, and day and night shall not cease.

— GENESIS 8:22

Be not deceived; God is not mocked: for whatsoever a man soweth, that shall he also reap.

— GALATIANS 6:7

CHAPTER FOUR

TO KILL AND TO HEAL

ON MANY LEVELS, even the most basic, over forty million people are unemployed, and millions lack health coverage.

CRIMINAL JUSTICE AND HEALTHCARE

This refers to the execution of criminals and the healing of the sick.

BIBLICAL EXAMPLES

Scriptures for reference:

- *Deuteronomy 13:6–10*
- *Luke 5:31*

The first murder recorded in the Bible occurs in Genesis 4:1–11, where flawed reasoning develops between two brothers, Cain and Abel. Cain becomes angry because God accepts his brother's offering but not his own. Although God counsels Cain, he allows his emotions to overwhelm him.

> *Be ye angry, and sin not: let not the sun go down upon your wrath.*
>
> — EPHESIANS 4:26

> *Be not hasty in thy spirit to be angry: for anger resteth in the bosom of fools.*
>
> — ECCLESIASTES 7:9

Satan, the enemy of all people, often instills harmful ideas in minds.

> *The thief cometh not, but for to steal, and to kill, and to destroy: I am come that they might have life, and that they might have it more abundantly.*
>
> — JOHN 10:10

We need God's love and wisdom to prevail in every troubling situation. Unfortunately, many don't love themselves or allow their emotions and environment to override sound judgment. We must understand God's love for us and our neighbors.

Drunk driving can cause death. Many lives are lost at the hands of others, leading to a high prison population and devastated families.

> *For if ye forgive men their trespasses, your*
> *heavenly Father will also forgive you:*
> *But if ye forgive not men their*
> *trespasses, neither will your Father*
> *forgive your trespasses.*

> — MATTHEW 6:14–15

Responsibility and self-awareness should guide our behavior. We should aim to do good and avoid evil.

God can help us heal from the deaths of loved ones. While it's not easy, we can find comfort and healing in Him, even during painful times.

> *I will not leave you comfortless: I will come*
> *to you.*

> — JOHN 14:18

God can also heal all manner of sickness. He may use a medical process involving doctors, surgeries, or medications.

We can inhibit our healing by neglecting prescribed medicines or failing to change our diets. Exercise, though beneficial many times, is not the ultimate cure.

> *For bodily exercise profiteth little: but*
> *godliness is profitable unto all things,*
> *having promise of the life that now is,*
> *and of that which is to come.*

— 1 TIMOTHY 4:8

Familial conditions may challenge us, requiring lifestyle adjustments to improve our quality of life. Refusal to change can extend suffering.

CHAPTER FIVE

TO BREAK DOWN AND BUILD UP

SIMPLY PUT, there is a time to tear down old, dilapidated buildings and replace them with new ones.

When you plant a seed, you must break the ground. Let us break the hardness of our hearts so they may open and let in the light. Let us shatter the blinders, illusions, and denial to move forward. We must dismantle the systems of racism and the stereotypes that sustain them. Let us break the chains of partisan division and the pervasive feeling that it's all just bad news. We must end the poverty and violence cycles that tear our nation apart.

We need God's help to effect meaningful change in every circumstance.

> *Except the Lord build the house, they labor*
> *in vain that build it: except the Lord*
> *keep the city, the watchman waketh*
> *but in vain.*

— PSALM 127:1

Change can be uncomfortable, but it is necessary to improve our quality of life—individually and as a nation. It requires a sacrifice of time, energy, and resources and often involves tough conversations.

We need God's wisdom to tackle the abovementioned issues and facilitate a season of meaningful change. Many people struggle with change; however, overcoming man-made barriers is essential for enhancing the quality of life. We must not let selfish agendas thwart what is best for the common good.

> *If any of you lack wisdom, let him ask of*
> *God, that giveth to all men liberally,*
> *and upbraideth not; and it shall be*
> *given him.*

— JAMES 1:5

Some people get mired in life's routines, but God established that growth requires adaptation from the beginning. We should constantly seek more effective ways to improve the world. Identifying the need for change and taking steps to implement it are crucial.

We make decisions that can help us adapt to new seasons. Fresh information and wise counsel can guide us toward beneficial changes.

> *A wise man will hear, and will increase learning; and a man of understanding shall attain unto wise counsels.*

— PROVERBS 1:5

> *Where no counsel is, the people fall: but in the multitude of counsellors there is safety.*

— PROVERBS 11:14

> *Let your speech be alway with grace, seasoned with salt, that ye may know how ye ought to answer every man.*

— COLOSSIANS 4:6

CHAPTER SIX

TO WEEP AND MOURN, AND TO LAUGH AND DANCE

WEEPING and mourning involve deep travail and anguish.

This Addresses the Feelings of the Heart
Good Times and Mourning

Mourning is the natural process of working through the heartache that follows a significant loss. It is normal and healthy to grieve for a period after a loved one has passed away. Ultimately, God uses mourning to produce healing.

Seasons of mourning serve a beneficial purpose—they remind us of our need to place our faith and hope in God: "Lord, remind me how brief my time on earth will be."

"Dance" is just as direct, meaning "to move in a pattern, usually to musical accompaniment." With this expressive coupling, Solomon contrasts a funeral gathering and a celebratory feast, such as a wedding. Humans weep and mourn at a funeral but laugh and dance at a wedding reception. Both good and bad times come into the lives of all.

Relevant Scripture

I am reminded of Romans 12:15–16: *"Rejoice with them that do rejoice, and weep with them that weep. Be of the same mind one toward another. Mind not high things, but condescend to men of low estate. Be not wise in your own conceits."*

We all will deal with some form of grief—whether at the loss of a family member, friend, coworker, job, dog, or possession. In these seasons of grief and pain, we must comfort one another with kind words of encouragement, visits, food, and monetary support. Checking on each other and offering hugs are also ways to provide comfort.

Everyone responds to grief differently, and recovery can vary in length. Many of us may have enjoyed laughter and dancing before our loss. God can settle us afterward, helping us hold on to good memories and restoring our laughter and dance. God can also assist us in refining our perspectives and outlooks.

Without God, life's problems offer no lasting solutions. The secret to peace is discovering, accepting, and appreciating God's perfect timing. Failing to trust God's timing can lead to despair, rebellion, or proceeding without His guidance. God will aid in our recovery and healing from the pain of loss.

> *I will lift up mine eyes unto the hills, from whence cometh my help. My help cometh from the Lord, which made heaven and earth.*
>
> — PSALM 121:1–2

> *For his anger endureth but a moment; in his favour is life: weeping may endure for a night, but joy cometh in the morning.*
>
> — PSALM 30:5

> *I will not leave you comfortless: I will come to you.*
>
> — JOHN 14:18

CHAPTER SEVEN

TO CAST AWAY STONES AND GATHER STONES

The Idea Is the Throwing Away to Clear a Field for Planting or the Gathering to Build a Fence
There Is a Time and Place for Everything

WE MUST EMBRACE change when it is needed. Change can help produce a better quality of life. It can be uncomfortable and almost always require a sacrifice—be it time, money, energy, partnership, vision, or a plan.

We need confidence, faith, determination, and diligence. Some people will embrace the vision before completion, while others will embrace it only afterward. Many struggle with change; some will not want to embrace change at all.

Sometimes, it may feel like you are walking alone with an idea for change. The question then arises: Are you a leader or a follower? Both leaders and followers are necessary, but understanding both roles is crucial for accomplishing anything.

Time can challenge one's perspective on an idea. Gathering money, resources, and the proper support can take time. We cannot let struggle or difficulty kill the dream. Instead, seek like-minded individuals and those with more experience to help push us into purpose.

Ideas should become realities, not dreams unrealized. Joy and a sense of accomplishment come when we actualize our ideas. Such accomplishment can fuel the birth of more great ideas.

We can build our track record and earn the confidence of others by achieving our goals. More support will come with time. We must be open to what God is saying as we move forward. Sensitivity to His leading will provide us with the best advice.

God can send the resources and the people we need in His timing. We can get into trouble if we move too quickly or too slowly. We must recognize opportunities and weigh their costs. We need people who will challenge our thinking positively—asking where we are going and how we plan to get there.

Greatness can be obtained through both small and great ideas. Hard work is not the enemy. Let's make room for more creative approaches by gathering new information and dreaming bigger.

CHAPTER EIGHT

TO EMBRACE AND TO REFRAIN FROM EMBRACING

This Refers to Illicit and Legitimate Love
Withdraw from Intimacy
and Should Not Always Be Taken in an Absolute Sense

- Malachi 1:2–3

The Bible Says

- Proverbs 5:18–21
- 1 Corinthians 7:2–5

GOD HAS GIVEN us limits to protect us and to preserve healthy relationships. How we live matters to God; how we treat one another also matters to Him. We should not want to lose His favor or blessings by disregarding what He has said in His Word concerning this matter.

> *Let no man say when he is tempted, "I am*
> *tempted of God": for God cannot be*
> *tempted with evil, neither tempteth he*
> *any man. But every man is tempted*
> *when he is drawn away of his own lust*
> *and enticed. Then, when lust hath*
> *conceived, it bringeth forth sin; and sin,*
> *when it is finished, bringeth forth*
> *death.*
>
> — JAMES 1:13–15

Love, when misused, becomes sin. We must pray and avoid situations that could lead to sin, seeking God's wisdom. Many families and relationships have been destroyed because of poor decisions in this area. Careers and reputations have also suffered because of abuses in this realm. Such behavior can contribute to the moral decay of any society; we must protect ourselves from giving in to temptation continually.

This behavior is often promoted through movies, songs, and commercials. Society encourages this conduct, but such behavior puts us at odds with God.

We should embrace family, friends, and strangers respectfully and without enticement. Caution is necessary to avoid misunderstandings, as our reputation is at stake. We must discern who can handle non-sexual embraces. Sexual intimacy should be reserved for husbands and wives.

Let us be good examples to those around us in this life area. God can help us exercise caution. Keeping temptation in check is crucial for our overall well-being.

CHAPTER NINE

TO SEEK AND KEEP, AND TO LOSE AND CAST AWAY

In Life, There Are Gains and Losses

The Wise Know When to Exert Energy in Pursuing Wealth and When It Is Prudent to Submit and Accept Loss

THERE ARE consequences for every decision. We must weigh the pros and cons of every choice; otherwise, what we lose may be more significant and more challenging to handle. Lessons can be gained through losses—what to do and what not to do.

Gains can help us overcome some losses. Effective management and budgeting are crucial. How many of our possessions slip through our fingers wasted?

We must manage all that we possess to preserve it. Some items may need replacement. Thinking about the past, the present, and the future is essential. Failure to plan is a plan for failure.

We live in an instant-gratification society. While there's a place for that, it cannot be a life rule.

We all will face losses—be it a poor investment, loss of a loved one, theft, or a natural disaster. We must manage and overcome these losses and keep going.

Sometimes, items must be cast away when something new and improved replaces them. Our quality of life can improve with necessary changes, although some people resist such changes.

The challenge lies in managing losses based on their nature. Evaluating our circle—friends, family, and coworkers—can reveal sources of loss. Adjustments may be necessary.

New information can change our outlook and perspective. Continuous learning is essential. The knowledge we gain and apply can impact our current season of life.

> *Where no counsel is, the people fall; but in the multitude of counselors, there is safety.*

— PROVERBS 11:14

> *Without counsel, purposes are disappointed; but in the multitude of counselors, they are established.*

— PROVERBS 15:22

*And we beseech you, brethren, to know
them which labor among you, and are
over you in the Lord, and admonish
you.*

— 1 THESSALONIANS 5:12

*If any of you lack wisdom, let him ask of
God, who giveth to all men liberally
and upbraideth not; and it shall be
given him.*

— JAMES 1:5

*Wisdom is the principal thing; therefore,
get wisdom; and with all thy getting,
get understanding.*

— PROVERBS 4:7

CHAPTER TEN
TO REND AND TO SEW

This is usually understood as rending garments as a sign of grief and repairing the tear when the mourning season ends.
Genesis 37:29, 34

DICTIONARY.COM DEFINES grief as "suffer disappointment, misfortune, or other trouble; fail." We all face challenges when confronted with grief. Prayer should be our refuge in seeking divine help to navigate and overcome such feelings. We should also seek comfort from individuals who can help us navigate the grieving process.

Grief can come and go and may be triggered by a memory—from a photograph, a conversation, a location, or even a family member. Consistent counseling could assist some people in recovering from their grief.

Grief is an emotion common to all humanity. It must be addressed, lest it hamper our quality of life and productivity. Sitting with the grieving and merely being present can sometimes be sufficient. Suggestions can be offered to the grieving to help them process information and make informed decisions. Understanding that people respond to grief differently is crucial. It's helpful to check in on the grieving person multiple times a week and set up a rotation of visitors or callers.

Comforting gestures—bringing food, flowers, and cards—can be helpful. Listening and paying attention to the grieving person's feelings can make a significant impact. Words of comfort and encouragement can go a long way.

Even during the darkest moments of grief, hope through Jesus Christ remains. Christ can provide solace to a grieving heart and mind. While life may never be the same, it is worth living. It's possible to recover and heal from grief.

The magnitude of grief often depends on the value placed on what was lost. Jesus Christ Himself related to this human experience as described in the Scriptures.

> *Then when Mary was come where Jesus*
> *was, and saw him, she fell down at his*
> *feet, saying unto him, Lord, if thou*
> *hadst been here, my brother had not*
> *died. When Jesus therefore saw her*

*weeping, and the Jews also weeping
which came with her, he groaned in the
spirit, and was troubled. And said,
Where have ye laid him? They said
unto him, Lord, come and see. Jesus
wept. Then said the Jews, Behold how
he loved him! And some of them said,
Could not this man, which opened the
eyes of the blind, have caused that even
this man should not have died? Jesus
therefore again groaning in himself
cometh to the grave. It was a cave, and
a stone lay upon it. Jesus said, Take ye
away the stone. Martha, the sister of
him that was dead, saith unto him,
Lord, by this time he stinketh: for he
hath been dead four days. Jesus saith
unto her, Said I not unto thee, that, if
thou wouldest believe, thou shouldest
see the glory of God? Then they took
away the stone from the place where
the dead was laid. And Jesus lifted up
his eyes, and said, Father, I thank thee
that thou hast heard me. And I knew
that thou hearest me always: but
because of the people which stand by I
said it, that they may believe that thou
hast sent me. And when he thus had
spoken, he cried with a loud voice,
Lazarus, come forth. And he that was*

dead came forth, bound hand and foot with graveclothes: and his face was bound about with a napkin. Jesus saith unto them, Loose him, and let him go.

— JOHN 11:32–44

I will not leave you comfortless: I will come to you.

— JOHN 14:18

Let us therefore come boldly unto the throne of grace, that we may obtain mercy, and find grace to help in time of need.

— HEBREWS 4:16

CHAPTER ELEVEN

TO BE SILENT AND TO SPEAK

Sometimes, we should speak out; other times, we should keep our mouths shut.

When we are not speaking, we are more inclined to open our ears—whether toward others or God. In our silence, we engage in self-reflection and obedience, which furthers our ability to listen to the Spirit.

SILENCE IS best in moments of anger. When we are angry, there's a high likelihood that the Holy Spirit will not inspire our words. James 1:19 instructs us, "Wherefore, my beloved brethren, let every man be swift to hear, slow to speak, slow to wrath." Similarly, "For he that will love life, and see good days, let him refrain his tongue from evil, and his lips that they speak no guile" (1 Peter 3:10).

Scripture tells us that silence can help us avoid sinning (Proverbs 10:19), gain respect (Proverbs 11:12), and is deemed wise and intelligent (Proverbs 17:28). You may be blessed by holding your tongue.

Ultimately, refraining from speaking in certain situations means we are practicing self-control. Maintaining our composure can be challenging. We should seek wisdom in controlling our tongue; when we control it, we ultimately walk by the Spirit. Self-control, a fruit of the Spirit (Galatians 5:22), is a blessed discipline.

Fear, a lack of self-confidence, and anxiety can tempt us to remain silent when we need to speak the truth boldly. But walking with the Lord means we must bring justice to the weak and fatherless (Psalm 82:3), correct oppression, speak wisdom (Psalm 37:30), and advocate for the widow (Isaiah 1:17). When we take a cowardly, quiet backseat to injustice, our silence does more harm than good.

If fear prevents us from sharing the gospel, our silence is more detrimental than helpful. Remember, *"As we were allowed of God to be put in trust with the gospel, even so we speak; not as pleasing men, but God, which trieth our hearts"* (1 Thessalonians 2:4). Just as the Lord told Paul in Acts 18:9, *"Be not afraid, but speak, and hold not thy peace,"* so must we heed the call to evangelize at the proper time and place.

And what should we speak of? We should speak the truth in love (Ephesians 4:15), put away falsehood (Ephesians 4:25), and speak truthfully in Christ

(Romans 9:1). When we express ourselves with godly clarity and truth, we are teaching and admonishing one another wisely (Colossians 3:16).

Just as Paul implored the church in Ephesus to pray for his boldness (Ephesians 6:18–20), we too should ask the Lord that "utterance may be given unto us, that we may open our mouths boldly, to make known the mystery of the gospel" (Ephesians 6:19).

In conclusion, the Holy Spirit will empower us when we are lacking: *"But ye shall receive power, after that the Holy Ghost is come upon you"* (Acts 1:8). In His great mercy, grace, and love, God grants believers the power to be effective. Today, pray and ask the Lord to remind you: *"And whatsoever ye do in word or deed, do all in the name of the Lord Jesus"* (Colossians 3:17).

For example:

> *A man hath joy by the answer of his mouth:*
> *and a word spoken in due season, how*
> *good is it!*

— PROVERBS 15:23

> *Even a fool, when he holdeth his peace, is*
> *counted wise: and he that shutteth his*
> *lips is esteemed a man of*
> *understanding*

— PROVERBS 17:28

*Wherefore, my beloved brethren, let every
man be swift to hear, slow to speak,
slow to wrath: For the wrath of man
worketh not the righteousness of God*

— JAMES 1:19–20

CHAPTER TWELVE

TO LOVE AND HAVE PEACE, AND TO HATE AND HAVE WAR

THESE ARE the fruits of human endeavor and other emotions, perhaps on the opposite end of the spectrum. Both emotions—love and hate—are common in life.

There are things to be loved (John 13:34-35). There are things to be hated (Proverbs 6:16-19).

Anger over the murder of George Floyd and the way other cops did nothing. Anger that this keeps happening. Anger at the looters. Anger at the agitators with malevolent purposes. Anger that people fuel the flames of hatred and division in our country. Hating what is happening to us. Hating the deterioration of a moral center. Hating that we are so divided as a nation. Hating that the Chinese and Russians are exploiting this and sowing division on the Internet. Hating that the faith we cling to and that guides us—the Word of

God—is so easily undermined that it can be used as a mere prop.

The lesson from this is that we should not depend on things over which we have no ultimate control.

We must also contemplate this in our sermon on Ecclesiastes 3. We know we are creatures of time by how we set our clocks and watches so that we will know what hour it is. We have schedules and appointments set by dates on a calendar. We know larger amounts of time by measuring the months and years. We also recognize the seasons: spring, summer, fall, and winter. But perhaps time should be measured in more than hours, days, or years.

MAN'S DUTY REGARDING THE TIMES AND SEASONS

Now is the time to prioritize time with the Lord. If you are always on the move, having quality time with the Lord is hard—if not impossible. Later in Ecclesiastes, Solomon says in Ecclesiastes 5:1-2:

> *Guard your steps when you go to the house of God. To draw near to listen is better than to offer the sacrifice of fools, for they do not know that they are doing evil. Be not rash with your mouth, nor let your heart be hasty to utter a word before God, for God is in heaven, and you are on earth. Therefore, let your words be few.*
>
> *Be still, and know that I am God.*
>
> — PSALM 46:10

These verses remind us of the importance of quieting our hearts before the Lord. Work on your prayer life. Prayer is not just asking God for things; it's about discussing life, seeking direction, and looking for understanding. It's simply talking to Him about your day.

Read good Christian books. Instead of reading only novels or self-help books, try reading a book that will help you grow in your relationship with Christ. Set a simple goal: perhaps one book this year that will help you grow in your faith. Maybe you are an avid reader, so set a goal of reading one book per quarter—four in total—that helps you grow in some area of your walk with God.

Ecclesiastes 3:9-15

1. Man needs to realize that everything has a purpose in God's overall scheme.
2. Man cannot fully appreciate the beauty of God's scheme because they cannot see the finished product.
3. The human view of life has been compared to looking at a bedspread from the underside, which appears only as rags, seams, and knotty strings. God sees the upper side of the beautiful pattern His hands have made.
4. To understand and accept the times and seasons of our lives, we must view things from eternity's perspective.
5. Man has to make the best of what he is dealt.
6. We face only what people of past generations have endured (1 Corinthians 10:13).

CHRISTIANS UNDERGO SIGNIFICANT CHANGES

First, we are blind, dead sinners; then, we are made alive. We discover more of our sinfulness, and God continues to change our hearts. God wants to make our hearts more like His.

CHANGE CAN BE GOOD.

1. Change stretches you.
2. It challenges you by causing you to grow through the trials and tribulations of life.
3. Change prevents boredom.

Are you the same person you were ten years ago? Five years ago? One year ago? Even though there are contradictory things, each has its place.

HOWEVER, GOD DOES NOT CHANGE (HEBREWS 13:8)

Imagine what it would be like if God were inconsistent.

What if He were kind one day and cruel the next?

Or oscillated between being merciful and judgmental? What if one day He answered our prayers and the next He did not?

I thank God that He is unchangeable.

This constancy means you can always rely on Him to be there and to do the right thing. He won't change His mind about you.

> *The righteous cry, and the Lord heareth,*
> *and delivereth them out of all their*
> *troubles. The Lord is nigh unto them*
> *that are of a broken heart; and saveth*
> *such as be of a contrite spirit.*

— PSALM 34:17–18

VERSE 11: GOD HAS SET EVERYTHING IN ITS TIME, SO ENJOY YOURSELF.

We can't escape His presence, no matter how hard we try. Therefore, we must accept His infinite nature compared to our finite existence. This will lead us to accept His sovereign rule rather than reject or rebel against His divine supremacy.

During seasons of trial, we risk blaming God for our suffering, complaining excessively, and becoming so myopic that we overlook His sovereignty. In these moments, we must remember the promises found in Scripture.

> *When thou passest through the waters, I*
> *will be with thee; and through the*
> *rivers, they shall not overflow thee:*
> *when thou walkest through the fire,*
> *thou shalt not be burned; neither shall*
> *the flame kindle upon thee. For I am*
> *the Lord thy God, the Holy One of*
> *Israel, thy Saviour.*

— ISAIAH 43:2–3A

For the followers of Christ, sanctification is the primary reason we experience joy, pain, blessings, and trials. Therefore, we must ready our hearts to face whatever comes, ensuring our faith is not undermined.

Happiness Redefined

- Happiness is a by-product of obedience to God.
- Instead of solely consuming, contribute to others' lives.
- Each season brings both opportunities and challenges.

TIME

- Seasons are time-bound, meaning they have defined start and end dates.

- Despite hardships, Scripture assures us that hope lies not in our abilities but in the Lord's provision and timing.

> *It is of the Lord's mercies that we are not consumed, because his compassions fail not. They are new every morning: great is thy faithfulness. The Lord is my portion, saith my soul; therefore will I hope in him. The Lord is good unto them that wait for him, to the soul that seeketh him. It is good that a man should both hope and quietly wait for the salvation of the Lord.*

> — LAMENTATIONS 3:22–26

In seasons of blessing, it's essential to give credit where it's due and proclaim the glory of God.

> *Praise ye the Lord. I will praise the Lord with my whole heart, in the assembly of the upright, and in the congregation. The works of the Lord are great, sought out of all them that have pleasure therein. His work is honourable and glorious: and his righteousness endureth for ever.*

> — PSALM 111:1–4

This season calls for decisions that will enhance our spiritual well-being. The seasons of our lives become more fulfilling when we remember the teachings in Ecclesiastes.

ATTITUDE

We must also be highly aware of our fleshly propensities to confuse God's provision with expectation and entitlement. God owes us nothing, and we must guard against thinking more highly of ourselves than we ought. For affirmation of this truth, look no further than Christ's teaching:

> *He spake this parable unto certain which trusted in themselves that they were righteous, and despised others: 'Two men went up into the temple to pray; the one a Pharisee, and the other a publican. The Pharisee stood and prayed thus with himself, 'God, I thank thee, that I am not as other men are, extortioners, unjust, adulterers, or even as this publican. I fast twice in the week, I give tithes of all that I possess.' And the publican, standing afar off, would not lift up so much as his eyes unto heaven, but smote upon his breast, saying, 'God be merciful to me a sinner.' I tell you, this man went down*

*to his house justified rather than the
other: for everyone that exalteth
himself shall be abased; and he that
humbleth himself shall be exalted*

— LUKE 18:9-14, KJV

Indeed, for everything, there is a season and a time for every matter under heaven. Undoubtedly, our seasons will be a mixed bag of blessings and trials, but our attitude must remain consistent, regardless of the season in which we find ourselves.

If we can find the silver lining God provides in our greatest trials, we will not be overcome by fear. God's greatest provision may be thorns that remind us not to live independently from Him but to depend solely on His sovereignty, just as Paul did.

And lest I should be exalted above measure through the abundance of the revelations, there was given to me a thorn in the flesh, the messenger of Satan to buffet me, lest I should be exalted above measure. For this thing I besought the Lord thrice, that it might depart from me. And he said unto me, 'My grace is sufficient for thee: for my strength is made perfect in weakness.' Most gladly, therefore, will I rather glory in my infirmities, that the power of Christ may rest upon me. Therefore I take pleasure in infirmities, in reproaches, in necessities, in persecutions, in distresses for Christ's sake: for when I am weak, then am I strong

— 2 CORINTHIANS 12:7-10, KJV

BOTTOM-LINE

If we learn to find blessings in trials and be aware of the trials in blessings, we will more readily embrace whatever season comes our way. We can trust in God's Word as our source of strength because *"The Lord is not slack concerning his promise, as some men count slackness; but is longsuffering to us-ward, not willing that any should perish, but that all should come to repentance"* (2 Peter 3:9, KJV).

He longs for intimacy with us and will spare no expense to pursue us to the ends of the earth because His love fuels His will for us. The seasons we face are merely a means of His sanctifying power and purpose in our lives if we submit to His authority and obey His Word without excuse or reservation.

So, I will leave you with the top ten things you won't have to worry about in the coming years:

- The Bible will still have the answers.
- Prayer will still work.
- The Holy Spirit will still move.
- God will still inhabit praise.
- There will still be anointed preaching.
- There will still be the singing of praise.
- God will still pour out blessings upon His people.
- There will be room at the cross for His children.
- Jesus loves you.
- Jesus still saves.

ABOUT THE AUTHOR

Kurt Broadnax is a multifaceted individual—an accomplished author, revered spiritual leader, and savvy content creator. As the Senior Pastor of Bread of Life Church in Harker Heights, Texas, a role he's held for six years, Kurt has positively impacted countless lives. He co-founded the church with his wife, Lady Janice Broadnax, in 2017, and it currently stands as a beacon of faith and community in Killeen.

Before embarking on his ministerial journey, Kurt dedicated fifteen years to military service as an enlisted and non-commissioned officer. He also worked for a decade as a veteran service representative. He is academically accomplished and holds associate degrees in Air Conditioning and General Studies from Central Texas College. He is a graduate of the ministry program at Texas Southwest Jurisdictional School of Ministry, Church of God in Christ, located in San Antonio, Texas.

In the literary world, Kurt has penned thought-provoking works such as "Love Is An Action Word" and "Love is Love Can." His most recent publication, "Seasons of Life," guides readers through life's challenges and spiritual landscapes. Celebrating 29 years of marriage and acting as a spiritual parent, Kurt taps into his own reservoir of life experiences and spiritual wisdom to enrich his readers and congregation alike.

Beyond the traditional platforms of church and print, Kurt is also a content creator across social media. He engages audiences on TikTok, Instagram, Snapchat, and Lemon8, providing snippets of wisdom, faith-based teachings, and motivational content.

Having called Killeen home since 2000, Kurt and Janice are fixtures in their community, deeply committed to making a broad impact within and beyond their church walls. Kurt Broadnax remains a vital voice in these challenging times, seamlessly blending traditional spiritual guidance with modern connection methods to spread empowering messages of love, redemption, and faith.

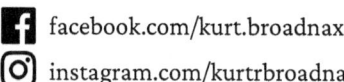

facebook.com/kurt.broadnax

instagram.com/kurtrbroadnax

x.com/KTBDX

ALSO BY KURT BROADNAX

Love Is An Action Word